Rupert, Polly, and Daisy

Rupert, Polly, and Daisy
by Jody Silver

Parents Magazine Press ● New York

To Stephanie C.
and my sister, Sue

Library of Congress Cataloging in Publication Data

Silver, Jody.
  Rupert, Polly, and Daisy.

  Summary: When Rupert seems to be paying more
attention to Daisy, the new fish, Polly, the bird, decides
to fly away.
  [1. Birds—Fiction.   2. Fish—Fiction.   3. Pets—
Fiction.   4. Friendship—Fiction]   I. Title.
PZ7.S5857Ru 1984   [E]   83-24979
ISBN 0-8193-1124-3

It was quite a day when Daisy
came to live with Rupert and Polly.
They fixed up a cozy spot for her
and watched as she swam about.

Rupert read to Polly
and to Daisy, too.

They sang
Polly's song.

Then they sang
Daisy's song.

When Daisy heard her song,
she started to dance!

Rupert was amazed and called
the neighbors in to watch.

As soon as Rupert realized
how clever Daisy was,
he taught her many things.

Then one day Rupert built Daisy
a castle to play in.
For the tower, he borrowed
Polly's bell.
Polly didn't like that at all.

Rupert tried to make
Polly feel better
by singing her a song.

Shoo fly,
don't bother me!
Shoo fly,
don't bother me!

Ding! Ding!

Suddenly, Daisy started
to play along!

Once again, Rupert ran
to get the neighbors.

This was more than Polly could stand.
Even though she knew Rupert would roar,
Polly reached into the fish bowl
to take back her bell.

But Daisy was not about to give up
the only sound she had ever made.
When Polly started to pull the bell up,
Daisy grabbed the string.

Polly knew Rupert would never forgive
her if anything happened to Daisy.

So she had to put back the bell.

When Rupert returned with the neighbors he began to sing as Daisy played along.

Meantime, Polly packed her things.

Just as Polly flew toward the window,
Daisy splashed Rupert.
Rupert turned his head in time
to see Polly fly away.

Rupert and the neighbors
ran after Polly.
But she was too fast and they
lost her at Town Square.

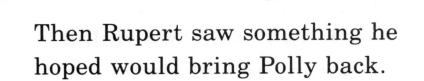

Then Rupert saw something he
hoped would bring Polly back.

He ran into Town Hall and
up to the bell tower.

Loudly, he rang out Polly's song.
All over town they heard it.

Polly heard it too
and flew into sight.

Polly flew near Rupert,
but she still was not sure
she wanted to go home.

As she backed farther
and farther away,
she could see that Rupert was
holding on by only a thin rope.

So Polly flew to Rupert.
Down below they cheered.

Then they sang Polly's song
while Rupert played along.

And together they went home.

As soon as Daisy saw Polly,
she flipped right up from her bowl.

Daisy was happy to see Polly.
And Polly was glad to see Daisy, too.

Rupert promised not to take any
of Polly's toys without asking first.

Then Rupert, Polly, and Daisy
danced and sang until it was time for bed.

About the Author

JODY SILVER has written and illustrated
several books for children, including
an earlier story about Rupert and Polly.
"Once I get to know my characters,
I keep thinking of new stories for them,"
she says.

This latest book is based on the author's
own feelings about having a new baby in
the family. "At first, I wasn't sure I liked
the idea of sharing things with my sister,
but now we get along well. In fact, I've
dedicated this book to her."

Jody Silver lives in New York City with
her husband and daughter.